D0606460

Whose Nose Is This?

A Look at Beaks, Snouts, and Trunks

Written by Peg Hall
Illustrated by Ken Landmark

Content Advisor: Julie Dunlap, Ph.D.

Reading Advisor: Lauren A. Liang, M.A.

Literacy Education, University of Minnesota

Minneapolis, Minnesota

Whose
Is It?

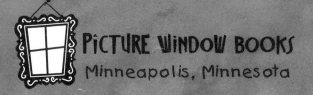

PICTURE WINDOW BOOKS
Minneapolis, Minnesota

Editor: Nadia Higgins
Designer: Melissa Voda
Page production: The Design Lab
The illustrations in this book were prepared digitally.

Printed in the United States of America.
1 2 3 4 5 6 08 07 06 05 04 03

Library of Congress Cataloging-in-Publication Data
Hall, Peg.
  Whose nose is this? : a look at beaks, snouts, and trunks / written by
Peg Hall; illustrated by Ken Landmark.
    p. cm. — (Whose is it?)
  Summary: Examines a variety of animal noses, noting how they look
different and function in different ways.
  ISBN 1-4048-0009-3 (lib. bdg. : alk. paper)
  1. Nose—Juvenile literature. [1. Nose. 2. Animals.] I. Landmark,
Ken, ill. II. Title.
  QL947 .H35 2003
  573.8'77—dc21   2002005776

Picture Window Books
5115 Excelsior Boulevard
Suite 232
Minneapolis, MN 55416
1-877-845-8392
www.picturewindowbooks.com

Are you nosy about noses?

Look carefully at an animal's nose, and it will tell you many things. Noses tell you how an animal eats or how it cools off in the heat. A nose might pick up food or dig in the mud. Some noses close up tight, and other noses poke into small places.

Most noses have nostrils for breathing and smelling. But noses don't all look alike, because they don't all work alike.

Let's get to know noses.

Look in the back for more fun facts about noses.

4

Whose nose is this, reaching for a leafy lunch?

This is an elephant's trunk.

The elephant sucks up water with its long trunk. Whoosh! It squirts the water into its mouth or down its back.

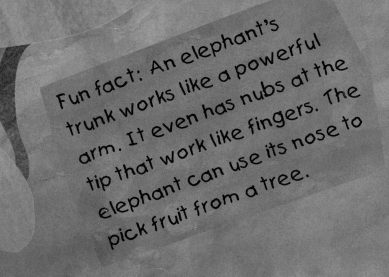

Fun fact: An elephant's trunk works like a powerful arm. It even has nubs at the tip that work like fingers. The elephant can use its nose to pick fruit from a tree.

This is a woodpecker's beak.

The woodpecker hunts for insects that live inside a tree. Tap! Tap! Tap! The woodpecker uses its beak to drill a hole in the tree, then gobbles up its dinner.

Fun fact: A beak is both a bird's nose and its mouth. A woodpecker eats with its beak and also breathes through two tiny nostrils at the base of the beak. Like most birds, woodpeckers have a very poor sense of smell.

Whose nose is this, stirring up the mud?

This is a platypus's bill.

The platypus closes up its eyes and ears and sticks its head into a river. The platypus uses its bill to feel for food along the muddy bottom. The tender bill can feel very small things.

Fun fact: A platypus's bill feels like rubber. It bends a little as the platypus digs in the mud.

Whose nose is this, closed up tight?

This is a camel's snout.

A camel's snout has amazing nostrils. The soft lining inside them helps to warm or cool the desert air. The long, thin nostrils can shut tight to keep out blowing sand.

Fun fact: A camel's nose can smell water from miles away. That's handy for an animal that lives in the dry desert.

Whose nose is this, sniffing in the dirt?

This is an anteater's snout.

The anteater sniffs around a pile of dirt.
If the anteater smells ants or termites
inside, it rips the mound open with
its claws.

Fun fact: An anteater has a
terrific sense of smell. Its nose
can smell 40 times better than
the average human nose.

Whose nose is this, hanging down so low?

This is an elephant seal's snout.

The male elephant seal takes deep breaths.
Its long snout fills up with air like a balloon.
When the air rushes out,
it makes a loud noise.

Fun fact: Male elephant seals make noise with their noses to tell other male seals to go away. The same loud noise makes female seals come closer.

Whose nose is this, poking out of the water?

This is a hippopotamus's snout.

A hippopotamus slips under water to keep cool in the heat. The hippo leaves its nostrils sticking out into the air so it can breathe.

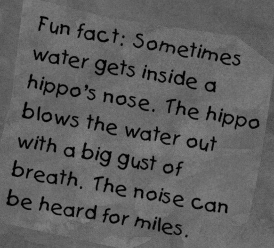

Fun fact: Sometimes water gets inside a hippo's nose. The hippo blows the water out with a big gust of breath. The noise can be heard for miles.

Whose nose is this, sniffing a flower?

This is your nose!

Your nose has tiny hairs inside it. These hairs catch dirt, and even tiny bugs, so you won't breathe them in. Your nose smells your food, just like the anteater's nose. Your nose warms or cools the air you breathe, just like a camel's snout. You can't close your nostrils like a camel, but you can hold your breath for a little while. Try it.

Fun fact: Your nose helps you taste your food. If you hold your nose shut with your fingers, food won't taste the same.

Just for Fun

Whose nose does what? Point to the picture of the animal described in each sentence.

elephant

elephant seal

woodpecker

camel

you

My nose closes up to keep out blowing sand.

My nose works like a hose for taking a bath.

My nose fills with air and makes a loud noise.

My nose catches bugs and dust.

My nose drills holes in trees.

Fun Facts About Noses

BIRD BEAKS The shape of the beak tells you important things about a bird. A bird with a long, thin beak finds its food by nosing into narrow places. A bird with a sharp, curved beak catches and eats animals such as mice.

SHARP NOSE When a baby alligator is ready to hatch, it rubs its snout back and forth inside the egg. A baby alligator has a small, sharp bump on the end of its snout. The sharp bump breaks the egg so the baby can crawl out.

FOLLOW THAT NOSE A dog's sense of smell is a million times keener than a human's. Dogs can smell things that you don't smell at all. That's why dogs are used to find people lost in the wilderness or trapped under mounds of snow.

UNDERGROUND STAR The star-nosed mole has 22 small fingers that fan out from its nose like a star's rays. The fingers, called tentacles, can wiggle and wave and dig through dirt.

BLOWHOLES A whale has a nostril in the top of its head. This special nostril, called a blowhole, lets the animal breathe while swimming near the surface of the ocean. Whales make noises deep inside their nose passages. The nose sounds echo through the water and help whales find food and other whales.

SMELLY BIRD The turkey vulture is one of the few birds that have a good sense of smell. Turkey vultures eat dead animals. They follow the rotten smell to find their food.

Words to Know

beak A beak is the part of a bird's body with nostrils and a mouth.

bill Bill is another word for a beak or for a platypus's nose.

hatch To hatch means to break out of an egg.

nostrils Nostrils are holes in the nose that let air go in and out.

snout A snout is a part of an animal's body with nostrils, lips, and a mouth.

tentacle A tentacle is a long, thin body part that moves like a finger.

termite A termite is an insect that often eats wood.

To Learn More

AT THE LIBRARY

Fowler, Allan. *Knowing About Noses.* New York: Children's Press, 1999.

Hartley, Karen, Chris MacRo, and Philip Taylor. *Smelling in Living Things.* Chicago: Heinemann Library, 2000.

Perkins, Al. *The Nose Book.* New York: Random House, 2002.

ON THE WEB

Lincoln Park Zoo

http://www.lpzoo.com

Explore the animals at the Lincoln Park Zoo.

San Diego Zoo

http://www.sandiegozoo.org

Learn about animals and their habitats.

Want to learn more about animal noses? Visit FACT HOUND at

http://www.facthound.com

Index